D1489606

RIGHT NOW!

Real Kids Speaking Up for Change

Written by Miranda Paul
Illustrated by Bea Jackson

CLARION BOOKS
Houghton Mifflin Harcourt
Boston   New York

CLARION BOOKS
3 Park Avenue
New York, New York 10016

Text copyright © 2021 by Miranda Paul
Illustrations copyright © 2021 by Brittany Jackson

All rights reserved. For information about permission to reproduce selections from this book,
write to trade.permissions@hmhco.com or to Permissions, Houghton Mifflin Harcourt Publishing
Company, 3 Park Avenue, 19th Floor, New York, New York 10016.

Clarion Books is an imprint of Houghton Mifflin Harcourt Publishing Company.

hmhbooks.com

The illustrations in this book were executed digitally.

The text was set in Bodoni Egyptian Pro.
Cover and interior design by Mary Claire Cruz

Library of Congress Cataloging-in-Publication Data is available.
ISBN 978-0-358-13732-0

Manufactured in China
SCP 10 9 8 7 6 5 4 3 2 1
4500823884

For Elizabeth,
and everyone who has
marched with our family.
—M.P.

For everyone who has shown me that as an
artist I have a voice in my gift—and with it,
I too can speak up.
—B.J.

Has anyone ever asked you:
What do you want to be when you grow up?

Here's a new question:

What do you want to do **right now**?

You don't have to wait
until you are big

And you can add your voice
to the chorus of brave young people
who have already paved the way.

SOPHIE CRUZ
Speaks Up for Families

A massive crowd gathers
to watch Pope Francis pass by.
A five-year-old moves closer,
slips past the barrier.
The guards seize her,
but the Pope lets this child come.

She hands him a letter
as cameras record.
She speaks words
filled with love for her family.
The world watches.

Five-year-old **Sophie Cruz**
ran past the crowds and cameras
to give Pope Francis a letter
about the fear and pain that
immigration laws can cause for
real families like hers that face
separation or deportation.

Sophie was later invited to
the White House and to speak
in several films and videos,
which have inspired many people
to work for immigration reform.

"Immigrants like my dad are good people. They deserve to come out of the shadows, so people can see how hard they work."

JONAS CORONA
Speaks Up for Those Experiencing Homelessness and Hunger

"Everyone should have what they need. If you have a lot, give a little. If you have a little, give your time."

"You're too young," people said
when you tried to help
those experiencing homelessness.
So your little hands
grabbed a pencil
and made a picture of what you saw:
kids waiting in long lines
for food and clothing—
but there weren't any clothes that fit.

Then those hands
collected and delivered four truckloads
of donations.
You marched to the shelter
every month
with your mama and aunt
to help kids look in the mirror
and love what they see.

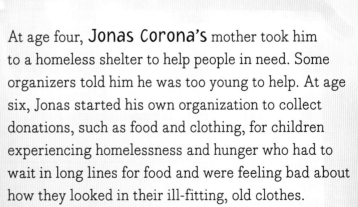

At age four, **Jonas Corona's** mother took him
to a homeless shelter to help people in need. Some
organizers told him he was too young to help. At age
six, Jonas started his own organization to collect
donations, such as food and clothing, for children
experiencing homelessness and hunger who had to
wait in long lines for food and were feeling bad about
how they looked in their ill-fitting, old clothes.

Jonas and his mother have appeared on television
shows to spread their message and inspire others to
act on the issues of homelessness and hunger.

MALALA YOUSAFZAI
Speaks Up for Girls

The Taliban said she can't watch TV.
Or listen to music. Or go to school.

So she logs on and blogs
to tell the world
what her life is like,
and how it should be.

She declares what's fair
and unfair.

They want her to stay silent.

She speaks.
Loudly.

She shows the world
the power
of an educated girl.

"We realize the importance of our voices only when we are silenced."

When forceful authorities banned girls from watching TV, going to school, and more, **Malala Yousafzai** ignored the rules and shared her story online. The authorities shot her—but she recovered and continued speaking out.

Malala became the youngest winner of a Nobel Peace Prize and started a global fund that works for a world where every girl can learn and lead.

JAYLEN ARNOLD
Speaks Up for Kids with Disabilities and Against Bullying

Jaylen went to school.
Like you, like me.

But sometimes
his body twisted,
his muscles ached,
his cries pierced the classroom.

Students didn't understand,
        so they said mean things . . .

And Jaylen spoke up,
shared the facts,
made wristbands,
rallied others,
and challenged audiences
        to become allies,
to have empathy.

We hear you, Jaylen.

We choose to spread kindness.

"You can call me
a loud voice for kids . . .
stick around . . . grow with me."

At age three, **Jaylen Arnold** was diagnosed with Tourette Syndrome, a condition that causes his body and voice to twitch or "tic" at any waking moment. Being bullied in school aggravated his tics so much, it made his body incredibly sore. After leaving that school, Jaylen launched an anti-bullying website and campaign at the age of eight.

People around the world started sharing his posters, lesson plans, and videos— all aimed at spreading understanding and kindness, especially toward kids with disabilities.

BANA ALABED
Speaks Up for Peace

What is it like
to run for your life,
barefoot,
down pitch-black streets
that you once laughed and played in?

What is it like
to watch cartoons with your baby brothers one minute,
and the next minute carry them down flights of stairs
to escape the blasts of an air raid?

What was Syria like, before the war?
What can we do to help?

Without your voice, Bana,
many people would not have thought
to ask such questions.

But your simple, courageous words
told us:
"I need peace."

Bana Alabed was seven when she used
her iPad to share her experiences as a child
living in the midst of war. Her photographs
and simple words demanding peace let
millions of people know what life was like
for her family before and after they became
refugees.

After leaving Syria, Bana published a
book that helped people understand how
war affects children and how they can help
bring peace to our world.

"We all have to help one another,
no matter what country we live in."

\# Stand with ALEPPO

PLease Stop the bombing and end the Siege

MILLIONS OF CHILDREN
Are Speaking Up for Voiceless Animals

CARTER & OLIVIA RIES
Helping cheetahs, rattlesnakes, pangolins, and other endangered animals

THOMAS PONCE
Helping dogs, cats, monkeys, and other animals who undergo scientific testing

HANNAH TESTA
Helping ocean animals

WILL & MATTHEW GLADSTONE
Helping blue-footed boobies

JOSIAH UTSCH & RIDGELY KELLY
Helping nautiluses

THE ANIMAL HERO KIDS

Lucia, Kimaya, Evan, Landon, Genesis,
Josie, Ian, Rilee, Khendall, Hannah

Helping farm and domesticated animals

"Anyone can make a difference.
If we can, you can too!"
—CARTER AND OLIVIA RIES

JAZZ JENNINGS
Speaks Up for Transgender Kids

When she was born,
the doctors thought she was a boy.
(It happens sometimes.)
But Jazz is a girl.
Call her she.

Can we go outside and play now?

"It's a boy!" the doctors shouted when Jazz Jennings was born, but she knew from a young age that she was a girl. She began speaking out at the age of two, and by kindergarten was able to enroll in school as a girl. Jazz bravely told her story about being transgender on national television.

Although she's faced many harsh words and wasn't allowed to play on girls' sports teams for a while, her activism led to trans kids being allowed to play soccer on United States Soccer Federation (USSF) teams. Jazz continues to speak out on behalf of transgender kids and people everywhere.

"I think what matters most is the person you are on the inside."

ANGELA ZHANG
Speaks Up for Science

Mix one part childhood curiosity,
one part Dad's encouragement,
and a thousand questions.
Let the potion steep for a few years
until it's got a steady voice bubbling up.
Sprinkle in failure
(a few times over),
and pour in buckets of determination,
until you cook up a great idea.
Yield: A possible cure for cancer.
Serves: Millions of patients worldwide.

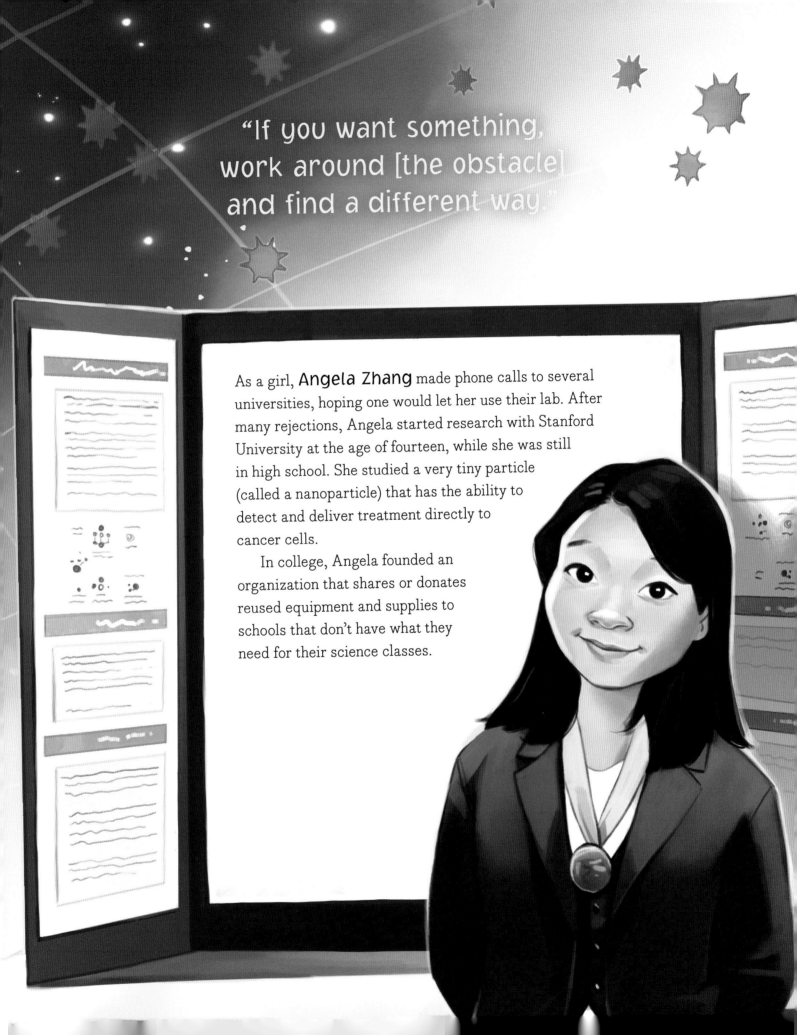

"If you want something, work around [the obstacle] and find a different way."

As a girl, **Angela Zhang** made phone calls to several universities, hoping one would let her use their lab. After many rejections, Angela started research with Stanford University at the age of fourteen, while she was still in high school. She studied a very tiny particle (called a nanoparticle) that has the ability to detect and deliver treatment directly to cancer cells.

In college, Angela founded an organization that shares or donates reused equipment and supplies to schools that don't have what they need for their science classes.

GRETA THUNBERG
Speaks Up for the Environment

A quiet girl
with her loud sign
sits alone
on giant steps.

Is anyone paying attention?

One year later,
from crowd to crowd,
and shore to shore,
and continent to continent,

her rallying cry echoes across planet Earth.

Our world is dying.

Our future is dying.

What must change?
Everything.

Who must act?
Everyone.

When?
Now, now, now.

"Instead of looking for hope,
look for action.
Then, and only then,
hope will come."

SKOLSTREJK FÖR KLIMATET *

* SCHOOL STRIKE FOR CLIMATE

Greta Thunberg was eight when she learned about climate change. She noticed that few people were discussing it or taking action. Over the next few years, she became very sad and ill, and even stopped talking—until it became absolutely necessary to speak.

Greta held her first climate strike alone outside a government building near her home in Sweden. She now speaks all over the world, demanding changes to laws that allow pollution and destruction of nature.

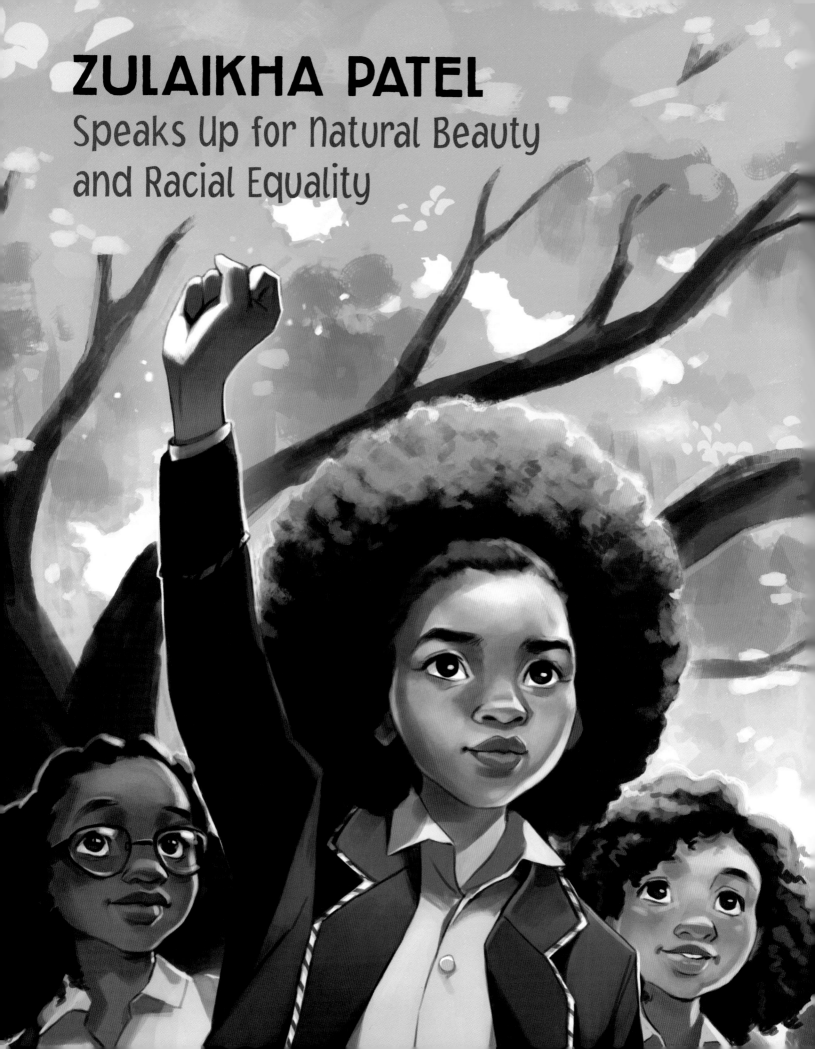

When her school told her she couldn't wear her hair
the way it grows,
so naturally fine and big and curly
atop her gorgeous Black head,
she spoke out.

Black hair is grand.
It is not dirty.
Black curls are exquisite.
They are not exotic.
A code of conduct shouldn't be
a code for discrimination.

Eye to eye with white police,
she raised her hands above her head,
willing to go to jail
to prove that Black is beautiful, brave, worthy.
She called into microphone
after microphone
to ask us to ride together
into a future of equality and justice.

"We know we
are beautiful
and occupying
every place."

Starting in elementary school,
Zulaikha Patel endured negative
comments about her Afro being "exotic"
or "dirty." At the age of thirteen, she
and her friends protested her school's
code of conduct, which required hair
like theirs to be cut, straightened, tied
back, or worn in plaits.

Their protest inspired their school
(and others in South Africa) to revise
its policies, and Zulaikha went on to
become an activist and speaker.

ROBBY NOVAK
Speaks Up for Everyone

Lights, camera, action!
A boy and his brother
film a playful video,
then another,
and another,
and another.
Joy! Laughter! Dancing! Singing!
A wise and silly Kid President
(sometimes wearing his swim trunks)
reminds us
to have fun, dream big,
and fill the world with love.

That's a wrap!

Robby Novak was eight when he made the first Kid President video, an idea that came from his brother-in-law Brad's belief that kids have voices worth listening to. Together, they filmed over a hundred videos that inspired people to laugh, be kind, and find joy.

After a three-year break, the brothers returned to YouTube with new videos that highlight other kids, especially those who are making the world a better place.

▶❙ 1:58/5:21

"Treat everybody
like it's their birthday."

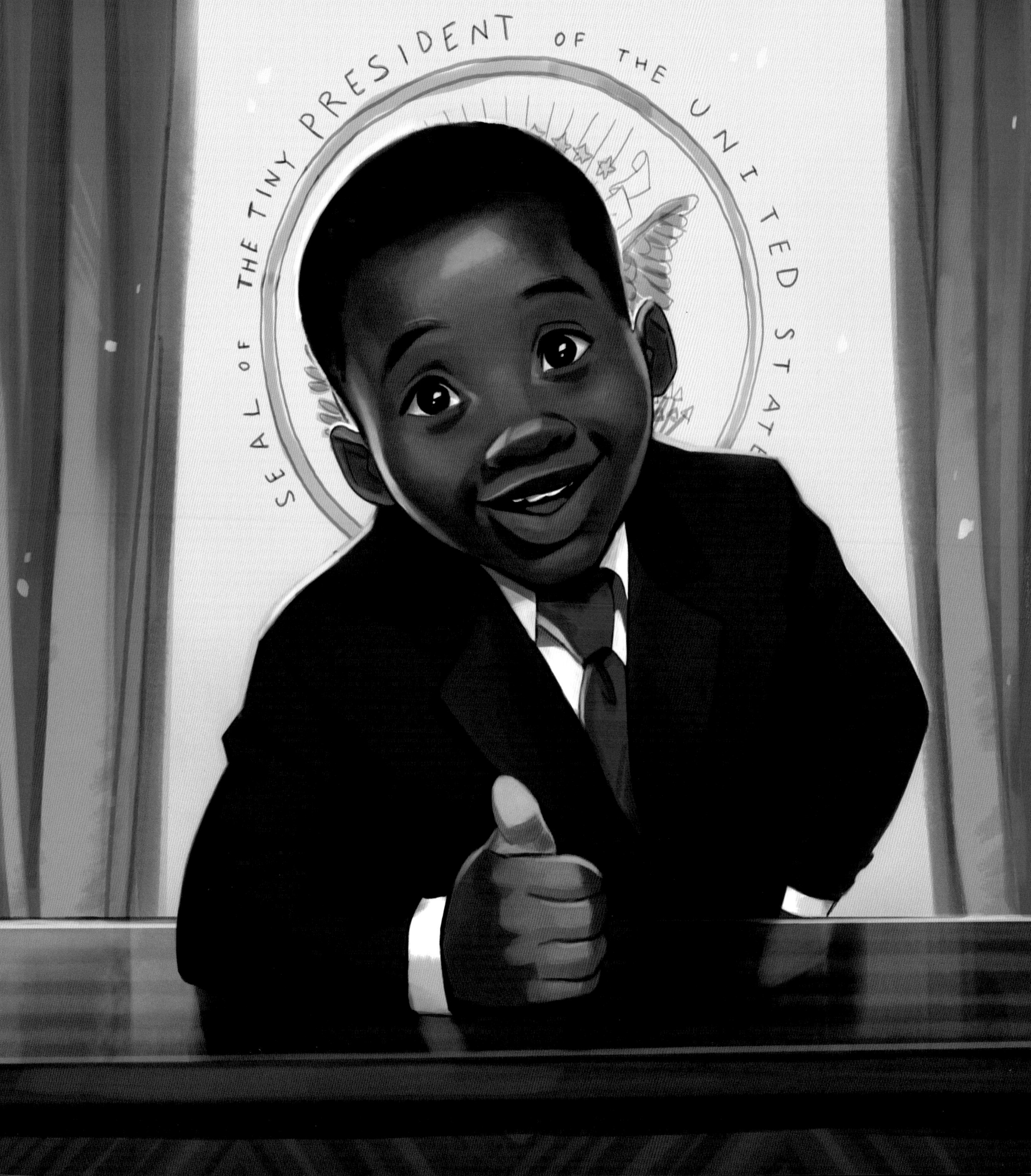

AUTHOR'S NOTE

Sometimes I hear complaints from grownups about "kids these days." But my research proves how extraordinary many contemporary kids are. I sifted through hundreds of stories of children making a difference, so writing a book that could highlight only a few of them became my biggest challenge. *Right Now!* showcases just a tiny slice of a growing population of young people doing incredible work.

As I researched, I noted how many of these activists had intersectional identities, which means they have been influenced or affected by more than one kind of lived experience that is marginalized by society. Many of these children have endured medical conditions, economic hardships, or cultural discrimination that makes their work challenging, but they find the resilience and motivation to help others in the face of those problems. They are shining examples of the greatness we can achieve when we put our minds, hearts, and voices into action.

I also learned that many children who speak up for change have supportive grownups in their lives. I'd like to praise all adults who encourage and work with young people. Although adults often look to young people with hope, it isn't the sole responsibility of children to solve the world's problems. We must all work together, young and old, to create the world in which we want to live.

YOU CAN SPEAK UP TOO!
ACTIONS TO MAKE A DIFFERENCE

What Can We Do to Speak Up for Families of Immigrants?

- Never refer to any human as "illegal" (only acts are illegal).
- Learn about immigration laws and send letters or make calls to local and state leaders.
- Volunteer for or donate to charities that help immigrant children and families.

What Can We Do to Speak Up for People Experiencing Homelessness and Hunger?

- Organize a drive for needed items or food in your area.
- Volunteer your time at a local homeless shelter or food pantry.
- Share your lunch (if allowed) or school supplies with classmates who don't have them.

What Can We Do to Speak Up for Girls?

- Recognize language that puts down girls and pledge to speak up when you hear it.
- Explore the Malala Fund's research library and Assembly newsletter.
- Collect money for girls' school fees or supplies.

What Can We Do to Speak Up for Kids with Disabilities and Against Bullying?

- Learn how to recognize bullying and practice phrases that you can use to call out bullying when you witness it, such as "That's not okay!" or "Stop now."
- Offer your friendship and kindness to classmates who have disabilities or kids who are alone.
- Share anti-bullying posters, lesson plans, and videos with teachers and classmates.

What Can We Do to Speak Up for Peace?

- Read books, listen to audio clips, or watch movies that show refugees' own stories.
- Learn how to take deep breaths so you can stay calm and help others instead of letting your anger turn into mean words or physical violence.
- Get to know your neighbors and reach out to new students or families in your communities.

What Can We Do to Speak Up for Animals?

- Participate in an Adopt-an-Animal program or wildlife event.
- Fight habitat destruction by recycling, using less water and energy, and generating less waste.
- Participate in citizen science efforts, such as animal counting or tagging.

What Can We Do to Speak Up for Transgender Kids?

- Choose not to label or think of certain colors or toys as "for boys" or "for girls."
- When someone tells you their pronouns, use them correctly.
- Interrupt if someone is laughing at or calling a transgender person a not-nice name or confusing their gender and let them know their words are hurtful.

What Can We Do to Speak Up for Science?

- Study science topics and practice innovation in a STEM lab or makerspace.
- Volunteer your time at a hospital or for a program that helps cancer patients.
- Raise funds or participate in a fundraising walk (such as a 5K) for medical research.

What Can We Do to Speak Up for the Environment?

- Read and learn all you can about climate change and environmental issues.
- Reduce your own impact on the earth—use less plastic, fossil fuels, and electricity.
- Plant trees, gardens, and native vegetation to help animals and ecosystems stay healthy.

What Can We Do to Speak Up for Natural Beauty and Racial Equality?

- Ask for books, dolls, and toys that feature all kinds of people, especially Black people.
- Don't touch anyone's hair, skin, or body unless they invite you to.
- Learn about racial injustice in history so we can better understand the issues of today.

What Can We Do to Speak Up for Everyone?

- Take care of and love yourself so you can be happy and do your best work.
- Remember that small acts are just as important as big deeds, and that every story matters.
- Dance and sing and laugh!

GLOSSARY

Activist · a person of any age who takes actions that will bring about change.

Ally · someone who helps and supports another person, group, or community—especially those who have been bullied or treated unfairly.

Climate change · a shift in land and weather conditions, such as how hot or dry a place becomes over a long stretch of time.

Climate strike · a protest to speak up for the environment led by students who walk out of or don't go to school.

Code of conduct · a set of rules at a school or workplace.

Deportation · when authorities send a person away from the country they are currently living in.

Discrimination · when one person or group treats another person or group differently than others, usually unfairly.

Ecosystem · all of the living and natural things found in the same area, such as a forest or coral reef.

Endangered animals · kinds of creatures that are at risk of becoming extinct.

Empathy · being able to respect, understand, and act kindly to others.

Gender · a label for social identities or community roles, such as being a boy, girl, or nonbinary.

Immigrant · someone who moves from one country to another to live.

Nanoparticle · a very tiny piece of matter, smaller than an atom, that can be seen only with a special microscope.

Plaits · another word for braids, cornrows, or woven strands of hair.

Pronoun · a short word that can stand in for a person, such as he, him, she, her, they, or them.

Racial equality · when people of all skin colors are treated fairly in all aspects of life, including by the government, at businesses, and in schools.

Refugee · a person searching for safety or shelter who has run away from danger or extreme hardship.

Transgender · when the way someone feels, expresses themselves, or identifies does not match the label (girl or boy) a nurse or doctor assigned them when they were born.

BIBLIOGRAPHY AND QUOTE SOURCES*

Alabed, Bana. *Dear World: A Syrian Girl's Story of War and Plea for Peace*. New York: Simon & Schuster, 2017. ✳ Page 104.

Animal Hero Kids. "Animal Hero Kids & Teen Crew." (animalherokids.org/animal-hero-kids-teens-crew; accessed July 11, 2019)

Blay, Zeba. "Watch 6-Year-Old Sophie Cruz Give One of the Best Speeches of the Women's March." Huffpost. January 21, 2017. (www .huffpost.com/entry/sophie-cruz_n_58839698e4b096b4a23201f6; accessed July 11, 2019)

The Blue Feet Foundation. "Our Mission." (bluefeetfoundation.com; accessed July 11, 2019)

Cirincione, Mary. "Cancer-Fighting Harvard Student Looks to a Future in STEM." *U.S. News & World Report*, May 12, 2015. (www .usnews.com/news/the-next-generation-of-stem/articles/2015/05/12/cancer-fighting-harvard-student-looks-forward-to-a-long-future-in-stem; accessed July 11, 2019) ✳

Corona, Jonas. "Jonas Corona on Serving the Homeless." Interview with Tamera Mowry, Jeannie Mai, Tamar Braxton, Adrienne

Bailon, and Loni Love. *The Real Daytime*. October 14, 2014. (www.youtube.com/watch?v=Avo02wZOuEQ; accessed July 11, 2019)
✴ Timestamp 0:45.

Dallman, Kasey. "Amazing Kids! of the Month—January 2013—Olivia and Carter Ries." *Amazing Kids Magazine*, January 2013. (mag.
amazing-kids.org/amazing-kids-of-the-month1/amazing-kids-of-the-month-january-2013-olivia-and-carter-ries; accessed July 11,
2019) ✴

Hannah 4 Change. "She Is on a Mission." (www.hannah4change.org; accessed July 11, 2019.)

Hernández, Arelis R. "Meet Sophie Cruz, 5-year-old Who Gave the Pope a Letter Because She Doesn't Want Her Parents Deported."
Washington Post, September 23, 2015. (www.washingtonpost.com/news/local/wp/2015/09/23/meet-the-5-year-old-who-gave-
the-pope-a-letter-because-she-doesnt-want-her-parents-deported; accessed July 11, 2019)

Jaylen's Challenge. "Who Is Jaylen?" (www.jaylenschallenge.org; accessed July 11, 2019) ✴ "Our Story"

Jennings, Jazz. *Being Jazz: My Life as a (Transgender) Teen*. New York: Crown Books for Young Readers, 2016.

Jennings, Jazz, and Herthel, Jessica. *I Am Jazz*. New York: Dial, 2014. ✴ Page 41.

Love in the Mirror. "Why Was Love in the Mirror Started?" (loveinthemirror.org/history; accessed July 11, 2019)

Magnone, Matt. "Guide to Being Awesome: Treat Everyone Like It's Their Birthday" Timestamp 0:27. Arcade Matt YouTube Channel.
(www.youtube.com/watch?v=Dw4SdqrPFqI; accessed October 6, 2020) ✴ Timestamp 0:27.

Malala Fund. "Malala's Story." (www.malala.org/malalas-story; accessed July 11, 2019)

Million Dollar Vegan. "Animal Hero Kids." (www.milliondollarvegan.com/the-kids; accessed July 11, 2019)

Mogoatlhe, Lerato. "Give Young People a Seat at the Decision-Making Table, Says South African Activist Zulaikha Patel." *Global
Citizen*, June 15, 2020. (www.globalcitizen.org/en/content/zulaikha-patel-youth-day-south-africa; accessed October 6, 2020) ✴

Montague, Brad, and Robby Novak. *Kid President's Guide to Being Awesome*. New York: HarperCollins, 2015.

Moton, Kenneth. "Meet the Little Girl Blessed by Pope Francis." ABC News. September 23, 2015. (www.abcnews.go.com/US/meet-
young-girl-blessed-pope-francis/story?id=33981305; accessed October 6, 2020) ✴

News24. "Four South Africa Women Make It on BBC's 100 Women List 2016." November 22, 2016. (www.news24.com/you/archive/
four-south-africa-women-make-it-on-bbcs-100-women-list-2016-20170728; accessed October 6, 2020)

Novak, Robby. "I Think We All Need a Pep Talk." TED Talk. January 2013. (www.ted.com/talks/kid_president_i_think_we_all_
need_a_pep_talk; accessed July 11, 2019)

One More Generation. "Our Story." (www.onemoregeneration.org/our-story; accessed July 11, 2019)

Peace Fund Radio. "Heroes: Jonas Corona." (www.radio.thepeacefund.org/heroes/jonas-corona; accessed July 11, 2019)

Ponce, Thomas. Lobby for Animals (website). (www.thomasponce.wixsite.com/lobby-for-animals; accessed July 11, 2019)

Save the Nautilus. "Our Mission: We Want to Raise Awareness about the Nautilus and Its Precarious Future." (www.savethenautilus.
com/about-us; accessed July 11, 2019)

Specia, Megan. "Bana al-Abed: From a Syrian War Zone to New York City. *New York Times*, October 6, 2017. (www.nytimes.com/
2017/10/06/world/middleeast/bana-alabed-aleppo-syria.html; accessed July 11, 2019)

Thunberg, Greta. "The Disarming Case to Act Right Now on Climate Change." TED Talk. November 2018. (www.ted.com/talks/
greta_thunberg_the_disarming_case_to_act_right_now_on_climate_change/transcript; accessed July 11, 2019) ✴ Timestamp
10:15.

Vilakazi, Thabile. "South African Students Protest against School's Alleged Racist Hair Policy." CNN. September 1, 2016. (www.cnn
.com/2016/08/31/africa/south-africa-school-racism/index.html; accessed July 11, 2019)

Walsh, Jim. "Transgender High-School Athlete to MSHSL: 'All Kids Deserve to be Happy.'" MinnPost.com. December 4, 2014. (www
.minnpost.com/sports/2014/12/transgender-high-school-athlete-mshsl-all-kids-deserve-be-happy; accessed July 11, 2019)

Witte, Brian. "Little Girl Is Star of Papal Parade." *U.S. News & World Report*, September 23, 2015. (www.usnews.com/news/politics/
articles/2015/09/23/little-girl-shares-immigration-message-with-pope; accessed July 11, 2019)

World of Children. "Honoree Jaylen Arnold." (www.worldofchildren.org/honoree/jaylen-arnold; accessed July 11, 2019)

Yousafzai, Malala, and Patricia McCormick. *I Am Malala: How One Girl Stood Up for Education and Changed the World (Young
Readers Edition)*. New York: Little, Brown and Company, 2015. ✴ Page 186.

Zhang, Angela. "After School Project: Finding a Cure for Cancer." TEDxSanJose. October 24, 2012. (www.tedxsanjoseca.org/angela-
zhang; accessed November 11, 2020)

✴ ✴ INDICATES QUOTE SOURCES